D0811282

Walking in the Ribble Valley

by
Cyril Spiby

on behalf of the Ramblers' Association
(Preston & Fylde Group)

DALESMAN BOOKS
1978

70p.

**THE DALESMAN PUBLISHING COMPANY LTD.,
CLAPHAM (via Lancaster), NORTH YORKSHIRE**

First published 1978

© Ramblers' Association (Preston & Fylde Group) 1978

ISBN: 0 85206 441 1

46031010

Printed in Great Britain by
GEORGE TODD & SON
Marlborough Street, Whitehaven.

CONTENTS

Cover design by J. J. Thomlinson
Maps by Harry Turner

FOREWORD

IT IS only a year since Cyril Spiby's **Walking In Central Lancashire** was published, and now here is another book of rambles from the same pen, written by popular demand. More and more people are becoming disillusioned with aimlessly motoring about the countryside and are turning to books of rambles to find what Lancashire really has to offer — the quiet fields, woods, riversides and fells that are so near to the big towns and yet so far from the sight, sounds and smells of mechanised transport.

As before, the 16 field-by-field, stile-by-stile route descriptions have been checked and double-checked by our team of volunteers, and this time we also include detailed maps kindly drawn for us by Harry Turner of the Furness Group of the R.A. The descriptions and the maps are sufficient to enable anyone to follow the walks, but you will find your enjoyment immensely increased if you also have the appropriate Ordnance Survey maps, and for that reason we again give the sheet numbers at the head of each walk.

All the routes in this book are on **definitive public paths.** This means that no-one has any right to prevent or discourage you from using them. In the unlikely event of this happening, or if you have any other problems connected with the walks, please write to us c/o the publishers enclosing a stamped addressed envelope if an answer is required. Our thanks are again due to the **Lancashire Evening Post** for allowing us to reprint a few walks which originally appeared in the successful series in "Leisure-post".

ALAN HOWARD,

**Chairman, Preston & Fylde Group
of the Ramblers' Association.**

A circular walk from New Hotel, Ribchester, via Shire burn House (alternatively, finish at Hurst Green 3¾ miles) 8 miles

Bus to New Hotel, Ribchester.   Map O.S. 2½" sheet SD 63.

CONFRONTATIONS between ramblers and highwaymen are not common these days, so relax and enjoy a walk through superb countryside that is spiced with an interesting assortment of links with the past.

New Hotel to Stydd Mill. New Hotel is on the Blackburn Road out of Ribchester and just beyond is a lane on the left on the nearside of Stone Bridge; this is Stydd (Stidd) Lane which is featured in walk No. 2 of this book.

For this walk, leave the lane as soon as you have crossed Boyce's Brook by turning right along a short length of track. This leads to a stiled gateway beyond which follow Stidd Brook halfway up the field before crossing it at a stone slab bridge, then continue upstream but following the right-hand hedge that is parallel to the stream. Cross another stiled gateway, then continue to a double stile on the right at the end of the field, avoiding a more prominent stile to the left; over the double stile, go forward to cross Duddel Brook at a footbridge.

Thus in so short a distance you have crossed three different brooks, which by the time they have reached Stone Bridge have united to flow the last quarter mile to the river Ribble. In the past these brooks provided power to run many small mills, mostly making bobbins for cotton mills; the remains of one such mill will be seen a little later. Stidd Brook on the west and Starling Brook on the east mark the boundaries of Dutton, an arrow-shaped parish with its point on the top of Longridge Fell to the north and its tail formed by the river Ribble in the south, roughly marked by the bridges of Ribchester and Dinckley; down the centre of the parish runs the beautiful wooded valley of Duddel Brook.

From the footbridge go left across the next field keeping along the top of a slight slope that leads to a stile; over this, the left-hand boundary leads to a stile in the next corner with Holmes Farm over to the right. Over the stile, go forward at first, then bear right to follow Duddel Brook which is over the banking on your left; pass by the slab bridge over the brook and walk on to cross a double stile in a sharp corner of the field. A few yards to the left another stile has to be crossed, then go forward and up a banking to join Gallows Lane at a stile on the right of a depression. Go left up the lane a short distance, past the first gate on the left to leave by a stile on the left by a gate where the road bends right. Go straight forward across the middle of the field to cross a double stile at a lower level, then along a pleasant grassy track to enter Duddel Wood by an unusual double stile.

Follow the path through the wood, faint at first but becoming more pronounced, to reach the ruins of the mill mentioned earlier, on the right-hand side; this was Stydd Mill which had the rare distinction of making combs. So well has nature clothed the ruins that it is possible to pass without noticing, but a little of their history is worth mentioning. Four sons of a local family named Charnock were orphaned, and two of them went to live on a farm at Brindle where it was customary for Spanish gypsies to camp. The Charnock brothers learnt from the gypsies the art of making combs from horns and subsequently put their knowledge to good use by building this mill; still living at Darwen is a Mr. C. Charnock, the only surviving member of the family with any experience of the craft. Bela Mill, Milnthorpe, is the next nearest comb mill and still carries on production; although horn is no longer used, the giant water-wheel still exists and was in use until about 10 years ago.

Continue past the ruins to a footbridge over Duddel Brook; do not cross, but a few yards beyond look for the path that doubles back uphill on the right-hand side above the old mill lodge. Near the top of the bank the path is lost amongst the trees and from this point I will give two routes to rejoin Gallows Lane; there is very little difference in the distance covered but if you are interested in places of note the first route I describe is for you as it goes by Dutton Hall.

Stydd Mill to Gallows Lane (Route 1). As I said, the path up the banking fades away but bear right to reach and climb a rail (stile needed) with a wall on your left that leads away from the wood to Dutton Hall (now a farmhouse),

No.1

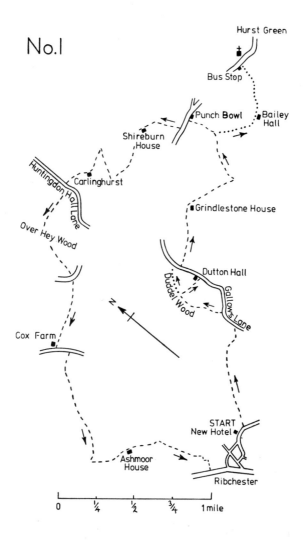

Hurst Green

Bus Stop

Bailey Hall

Punch Bowl

Shireburn House

Carlinghurst

Huntingdon Hall Lane

Over Hey Wood

Grindlestone House

Dutton Hall

Duddel Wood

Gallows Lane

Cox Farm

N

START
New Hotel

Ashmoor House

Ribchester

0   ¼   ½   ¾   1 mile

7

erected by Richard Townley about 1670-80. Even those people with as scant a knowledge of architecture as myself will find the building interesting. On the roof is a small wooden structure, the remains of a bell turret. The iron gates, fine as they are, have replaced the original wooden ones which were surmounted by a pair of quaint carved lions; I understand that looking from the gate, the right-hand side of the building is the older.

A gate leads into the yard where you go forward, then turn right and then left to pass by the gates referred to and reach Gallows Lane. Follow the lane to the left for a little over 200 yards to a gate on the right near what could be the site of an old small quarry. I will now describe the alternative way to reach this place.

Stydd Mill to Gallows Lane (Route 2). After climbing the bank above the old lodge as already described, instead of bearing right as in route 1, look closely to the left to detect a narrow path through the ferns and trees that leads up to a stile to enter the bottom of a sloping field. Go across the field and then, when a gate near farm buildings comes into view (a little over half-way along the top side), aim for it to reach Gallows Lane. (By rights there should be a stile to the left in the field corner). Go right along the lane for over 100 yards to reach a gate on the left which is the one already mentioned and marks the end of the alternative.

Gallows Lane to Shireburn House. Through the gate go forward and up, passing to the right of the quarry, to a stile on the left over which turn right. Follow the right-hand hedge through three fields and the left-hand hedge through two more fields to reach Starling Lane via Grindle-stone Farmyard; grindle stone is a north country term for grindstone which suggests that stone quarried in this area was used for that purpose.

Go right along Starling Lane for a third of a mile (there is a wooden gate to pass through part way along) to reach a stile in an iron-railed fence on your left; this leads to a footbridge that takes you out of Dutton parish into the parish of Aighton, Bailey and Chaigley as you cross Starling Brook. A path, which may be screened by foliage in summer, climbs to a stile at the top of the bank. Continue forward across a large field that slopes up steeply to the right of a depression, and move gradually away from the depression to cross the stile in the top side. Keep the same direction to pass a low hill on your left to reach a farm road cutting across your route. If you wish to finish the walk at Hurst Green, turn to page 11 where you will find the route described.

For the circular route, turn left along the farm road to pass delightful Titum Cottage and reach the Hurst Green road with the Punch Bowl Inn, dated 1793, to your right. A highwayman by the name of Tom King is reputed to have taken refuge in this inn. Eventually he was captured and is said to have been hung on the gallows in Gallows Lane; his ghost apparently haunted the musicians' gallery in the dining room until it was exorcised in 1942 by a priest from Stonyhurst College.

Go left up the road, away from the Punch Bowl, to the cottages on the right known as Bailey Green. A farm road doubles back across the front of the cottages and you follow it until you come to Shireburn House on the left with its pretty garden.

Shireburn House to Cox Farm. Go through the gate on the right of the house gate and over a piece of soft and overgrown ground to pass through the right-hand gate ahead. Now follow the new wire fence on your left (and remains of an old fence) that leads straight ahead from the gates to cross a stile at a ditch. Aim for the right-hand side of Starling Bridge Wood ahead to climb the stile close to the wood. Your next stile is to the right in the fence running along the top of the field; the correct way is not to go diagonally but first to cross the field, then turn right to reach the stile. From this stile there is an excellent view of a wooded, undulating section of Longridge Fell.

Beyond the stile go forward, passing the tip of Carlinghurst Wood on your right. Then, when you are over the slight rise, turn left following around the base of a small hill to reach the farm road on the right-hand side of Carlinghurst Farm at a stiled gateway; you are now back in Dutton parish. Follow the farm road to the right to reach Huntingdon Hall Lane at Lane Ends. Almost opposite, a short length of track leads to a cottage where you enter the garden at a small wooden gate and go to the right-hand side of the cottage to cross a stile on the left of a greenhouse.

Over the next field is a double stile to the right of the left-hand corner, beyond which bear slightly right to cross a stile on the left of a gate. As you cross straight over the next field look for a small wooden gate that gives access into Over Hey Wood; if you come to a small iron gate you have gone too far left. A short length of path leads down a steep wooded bank on to the drive of Dutton Manor; go left along this to a kissing-gate on the right immediately after crossing the bridge over Duddel Brook. Through the gate incline left up the slope of the field, then at the top of the rise you will see Moor Cock Farm on your right front. Your aim is to pass to the left of the farm through a gap in the fence. After crossing a depression you reach the Hurst Green road at a stile in the hedge ahead.

Your way continues on the opposite side of the road but take care as you are on a bad bend; no doubt the footpath you are using existed long before the petrol engine was invented and the only danger in crossing the road then was from — Tom King? Having crossed the road safely with your life and valuables, cross the stile on the right of a gate. Do not go down the farm road but turn right to go straight across the field to a stile next to the left-hand tree of a clump. Continue in the same direction across the next field to climb a double stile in two wire fences and, still keeping the same direction, cross a line of trees. These trees go right to meet Stidd Brook in a dip; your aim is to bear right to cross the brook by a footbridge nearly 100 yards downstream to re-enter Ribchester parish. Cox Farm is ahead and you aim to the left-hand side of it to cross a tributary of Stidd Brook at a plank bridge, then reach Stoneygate Lane at a small gate on the left of the farm.

Cox Farm to Ribchester. Stoneygate Lane is on the line of a Roman road and you follow it to the left for 150 yards before turning down a farm road on the right; this leads past a renovated house on your left, through an iron gate, past Old Buckley Farm, and over a stone stile on the left-hand side of another iron gate to enter a field. Cut diagonally across the field, leaving it in the far corner at a gap; then keep the same direction in the next field, cutting across a very small corner to reach a stile in a fence after crossing a track and passing by an oak tree.

After crossing the stile, stand with your back square to it, then go directly forward across the field to a stile in a fence a few yards to the left of a group of trees that encircle a depression. Bear left slightly in the next field to leave at a stiled gateway. On your right you now have a shallow dry ditch, the site of an old hedge line and this angles away to the right. Keep this on your right, but gradually bear away to reach an isolated stone post on the line of another old hedge line. Just beyond this, a sunken rutted track starts and winds its way downhill to Boyce's Brook; on the right is a footbridge over the brook, do not cross but turn left alongside the stream.

Although lying close to the main Longridge to Ribchester road, this valley will come as a surprise to many as it is well concealed from the road. After crossing a footbridge over a tributary, follow a faint path as it inclines left to the top of the bank. Ahead you will see Ashmoor House; you pass this on the right-hand side after crossing a stile to join a track which you follow through two fields. At the end of the second field there is a stiled gateway; do not cross this but cross the stiled gateway on your right with Ribblesdale Mill chimney directly ahead. Go to the bottom of a long sloping field to cross Boyce's Brook at a concrete slab bridge, then cross the stile beyond. This leads onto a track alongside the right-hand side of the mill to reach the road at Ribchester; the Preston bus stop is to the left on the far side of the road.

Alternative route to finish at Hurst Green. Follow the farm road that cuts across, to the right, to reach Bailey Hall Farm; part of this is 16th century and there is a trace of a moat. Enter the yard and you will see, enclosed by a fence in front of the house, the remains of Bailey Chapel, founded by Sir Richard de Cliderhoe and destroyed in 1830. A portion of the north wall remains as do some steps leading down to a small vault; one of the salvaged windows has been built into the front of Stonyhurst College.

At Bailey Hall Farm turn left through a wooden gate and right through a second gate, to pass to the left of the remains of Bailey Chapel. Bear right along the traces of a sunken grass path that goes through some trees and to the left of a large beech tree, to reach a stile leading into Bailey Hall Wood. In the wood, bear left along a handrailed path that leads down to a footbridge over Dene Brook.

11

Some crude steps climb the opposite bank to a small iron gate, through which keep straight on up the bank to leave the wood and in quick succession cross a narrow strip of grass and a strip of ferns. Aim to the left-hand end of a hedge that comes in from the right, then head for St. John the Evangelist Church, Hurst Green. Join a farm road on the left at Merrick Hall (said to be the priest house of Bailey Chapel) which leads to the road opposite the church. Hurst Green is ¼ mile to the right; alternatively, the Preston bus stop is just to the left.

No. 2   TIME TO STAND AND STARE

A Circular walk from New Hotel, Ribchester, via Hurst Green.   **8½ miles**

Bus to New Hotel, Ribchester.   Map O.S. 2½" sheet SD 63.

RIBCHESTER and Hurst Green are two places worth visiting in their own right; one for its Roman connection, old cottages and riverside setting, the other for its close proximity to Stonyhurst College and the deep wooded valley of Dene Brook. Between these two villages lies some of the most beautiful and unspoiled countryside in Lancashire, which is so full of places where you will want to stand and stare that it will take many visits fully to appreciate it.

New Hotel to Greengore. New Hotel is on the Blackburn road out of Ribchester and just beyond is a lane on the left on the nearside of Stone Bridge. This is Stydd Lane and takes you past the little school on the right and St. Peter and Paul church and almshouses on the left. The almshouses were endowed by John Shireburne in 1726 for five persons (Roman Catholic widows or spinsters) to live separately, with coals and allowances. These terms are still adhered to.

After crossing Stidd Brook, the way continues as a farm road and takes you past the ancient Stidd (Stydd) church, one of the most interesting structures in the county. It was built by the Knights Hospitallers of Wakefield in 1136 and endowed with 11 farms. Points of interest are the Norman doorway and windows on the north side. The south doorway is Early English with waterleaf on the capitals. The church has a Jacobean pulpit with the remains

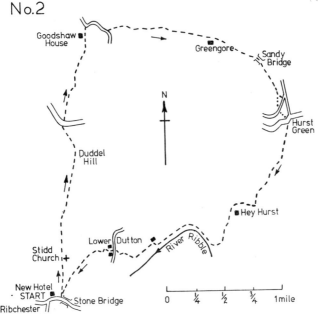

Goodshaw House
Greengore
Sandy Bridge
N
Hurst Green
Duddel Hill
Hey Hurst
Lower Dutton
River Ribble
Stidd Church
New Hotel
START
Ribchester
Stone Bridge

0   ¼   ½   ¾   1mile

of a canopy. Against the wall are some rough oak benches, the only seating available in that time. Upon these would sit the aged and infirm, giving birth to the saying: 'The weakest always go to the wall'. The church was restored in 1925.

Go straight across the yard of Stidd Manor Farm, passing through two gates and up the right-hand edge of the small field beyond. Go up the slope of the next field to a stile in the top right-hand corner. Continue uphill after this to cross a footbridge a few yards from the left-hand corner (in the corner is a large boulder; the remains of a cross). Keep on uphill to pass through a facing gateway, near the left-hand corner, then incline slightly right, up the middle of the next field, to leave by a kissing-gate on the left of a short length of stone wall. Make to the right of Duddel Hill summit with its remains of a cross. After passing over the hill, a farm road is joined at Duddel Farm, which is followed to the Hurst Green road at Dean Brow.

Cross the stile on the opposite side of the road and go

13

forward to pass through a muddy gap in a fence with the 17th century Moor Cock Farm over on the left. The gap is beside an oak tree and as you pass through you will see a small field of hen cabins 20 yards to your left. Keep forward up the rising ground, gradually closing in on Dutton Manor drive on the right. This is reached at a kissing-gate in a corner, after dropping down a short distance. Go left to cross Duddel Brook, then after a few yards turn right, where a path goes up a wooded slope to enter a field at another kissing-gate. Go left alongside a wood, uphill, through three fields, getting a glimpse of Dutton Manor through the trees on the left. In the third field a track that has started bends left out of the field, crossing a tributary of Duddel Brook. Follow this track past Goodshaw House Farm to reach the road near Low House on your left.

Go right along the road which bends left, right, left and right. At this last bend, cross the stile on the left by the left-hand of two gates. Follow the right-hand fence which bends right, gradually climbing, then levelling out alongside a stone wall to reach a prominent stile over another wall to the left of the field corner. Ahead is a good view, with Crowshaw Lodge in the foreground and Pendle Hill dominating the background. Go downhill in the direction of Pendle to a gate in the right-hand corner. Then go right, alongside the left-hand wall. This is a track, but it is not very evident at first owing to the boggy nature of the ground, and it brings you after nearly $\frac{1}{2}$ mile to the ancient Greengore Farm, part of which is 15th century.

Greengore to Hurst Green. After passing the farm, the track bends right; then a short way after, turn left, down a green track between a wall and a fence. After a while this leads down through Mill Wood to reach Sandy Bridge over Dene Brook. The last section of the track before reaching the bridge is very rough and overgrown and a worn path that goes off left indicates that most people opt to reach the bridge by a slight diversion. Cross the bridge and follow the downstream path through Mill Wood. When it starts to climb and leave the stream, look for an overgrown path on the right, to keep near the brook. The garden fence of Isle Cottage is passed on the right and the way becomes metalled, bending left uphill. Leave this track by a faint path that goes off right at the start of the

14

hill, alongside another right-hand garden fence, to reach another metalled road at some garages. (If you wish to do the next part of the walk via Hurst Green village, follow this road uphill to reach Avenue Road opposite the Bailey Arms. Turn right, passing the end of The Dene, then turn right again passing Shireburn Arms to reach Lambing Clough Lane on the left).

If you prefer the alternative, leave the road by the garages; a tarmac path goes off on the right. The attractive cottage down to the right is a renovated bobbin mill. The path takes you past the rear of Quality Row, then joins a wider track, bringing you to the road called The Dene. Cross the road and climb the grass bank opposite alongside a left-hand hedge. The way becomes enclosed, taking you through to Longridge Road. (Notice the ancient cross on the far side of the pair of houses before reaching the road). Cross over Longridge Road, then continue down Lambing Clough Lane a few yards to the left, signposted 'Dinckley Ferry'.

Hurst Green to Stone Bridge. After a third of a mile, Lambing Clough Farm is reached, just after which the track bends left. Go right, down a sloping field. Aim to a point where the wooded valley of Dene Brook, coming in from the right, meets the band of trees coming down the slope of the small hill on the left. Look for a track in the right-hand corner that goes downhill through a narrow neck of Merrick's Wood to reach a clearing, with a chalet on your left. Keep to the right of the clearing to reach and cross a footbridge over Dene Brook with a well-made stone bridge just upstream. Incline left, then right up the far bank, along a faint path, passing close to the second of two wooden bungalows on the right. Continue across the slope of the field, keeping the shallow dry valley on the left, to a stile between an oak and an ash. Keep forward in the next field, before turning left near the end to cross a ridge on the left. A cutting runs through this ridge, a most curious feature in such an unlikely spot. The story goes back to 1846 when the Fleetwood, Preston and West Riding Railway Company bought the Preston-Longridge line and had plans to extend it into Yorkshire. Work was started as this cutting shows, but opposition from the land-owners caused the scheme to be abandoned.

After crossing the end of the cutting, make for the bottom right-hand corner, where a footbridge on the right takes you over Starling Brook. Follow the right-hand hedge up and around two sides of the next field to meet the farm road to Hey Hurst, the farm down to your left. Cross to a stile a few yards to your right; then over this, incline away from the right-hand hedge, slightly downhill to a stiled gateway. Go forward, slanting downhill, to pass close by a boggy dip and field corner jutting out on the right, to a gateway in the fence ahead. A tall wooden stile stands uselessly in a line of trees just beyond. Follow a cattle-trod slightly left up the slope; as you pass over the brow bear right to cross a line of old trees to the right of a small dried-up pond at a junction of old ditches. Bear slightly right across the field. This should bring you to a low ridge about 70 yards from the river Ribble with Copy Scar Wood on your immediate left. Go right for a short distance parallel to the river, then drop down the slope towards the river to enter Haugh Wood at a stile.

Follow the riverside path downstream, leaving the wood after crossing a footbridge and stile. The path continues, passing Stewart's Wood and a smaller one, then leave the river to enter the yard of Dewhurst House Farm at a small wooden gate. Turn left down the farm road, passing the house. When the road bends left, cross the wide grass verge on the right to a stile tucked into a corner. Follow the right-hand hedge as it curves around, crossing two stiles before passing through the hedge itself via a double stile, to follow on the other side to reach Gallows Lane. Cross straight over to pass between the cottages of Lower Dutton, then bear right in the narrow field beyond to the left-hand of two stiles at the top of the field. Over this, go left to follow Duddel Brook on your right, but go left before reaching the end of the field to cross a stile in a wooden fence. Follow the right-hand hedge, keeping the same direction in the next field to reach a footbridge in the corner that takes you over Duddel Brook. Go forward to cross two consecutive stiles, then turn left down a narrowing field. After a stile, go forward before crossing Stidd Brook on your right. Turn left to the end of another narrowing field, where a stile leads onto Stydd Lane and your starting point is to the left.

De Tabley Arms to Edisford Bridge, via Whalley Abbey
(shorter version finishing at Whalley 6½ miles)   10½ miles

Blackburn bus via Ribchester to De Tabley Arms. Maps O.S. 2½" sheets SD 63, 73 and 74.

ONCE the road has been left behind, you enter a stretch of the Ribble Valley that will stand comparison with scenery anywhere else in the country.   Because there has not been a replacement of the river crossing since Hacking Boat ceased to operate, a detour is necessary, but this enables you to visit the remains of Whalley Abbey.   There are reminders on this walk of different types of battles that have been fought.   Some serve as a warning that our countryside and the right to walk through it cannot be taken for granted.

De Tabley Arms to Craven Fold.   De Tabley Arms is about 1 mile beyond Ribchester on the far side of Ribchester bridge (built 1774).   Walk back to the bridge from the inn and follow the road that goes alongside the river Ribble a short way, before bending away after crossing Connerie bridge, and reaches Salesbury Hall after 1 mile.   The road bends left at this large plain farmhouse, then bends right, uphill.   At the top of the bank on the left-hand side of this bend, a stile leads into Marles Wood, commonly known as Sale Wheel Wood.   A path, enclosed between wire fences, leads downhill, crosses a footbridge and reaches the riverside.

Sale Wheel is the name of the wide expanse of the river where the current has a circular motion caused by the flow of water after leaving a narrow stretch.   It is thought that the name is of Old English origin : Salh — 'Sallow, willow' and weal — 'whirlpool'.   Whilst absorbing the beauty of this place it is worth remembering an occasion in 1894 when the footpath through the wood was disputed, with the result that 'a crowd of about 1,500 well-dressed people, led by a few public-spirited gentlemen from Blackburn, visited the locality and asserted their right of way by walking the entire length of the path and removing all obstructions'. A more recent threat in 1959 was an attempt to create a caravan park beside the river; this was successfully opposed.

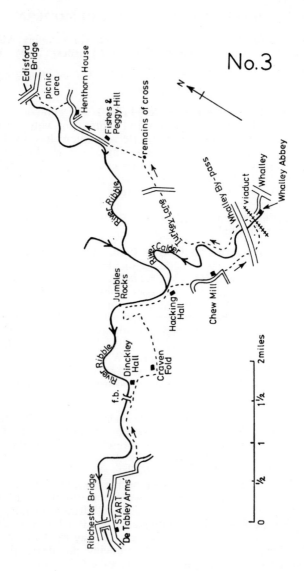

No.3

Edisford Bridge
picnic area
Henthorn House
Fishes & Peggy Hill
remains of cross
River Ribble
Whalley By-pass
viaduct
Whalley
Whalley Abbey
Turkey Lane
River Calder
Jumbles Rocks
Hacking Hall
Chew Mill
River Ribble
Dinckley Hall
Craven Fold
f.b.
Ribchester Bridge
START
De Tabley Arms'

N

0   ½   1   1½   2miles

18

Follow the worn path through the wood to a field where a line of boulders marks the route, then keep fairly close to the river to reach Dinckley footbridge, the successor to the old ferry that operated from Trough House across the river. Do not cross the bridge but join a track a short distance from the river which goes forward to a stile by a gate, beyond which the track continues towards the white-washed Dinckley Hall, said to be 600 years old. When you reach the junction with the access road, turn right, away from the farm, and follow the road up a wooded bank. Look out for a stile by a gate on the left, just before the gate across the access road. Over this you will have Dinckley Wood on your left; keep forward in a straight line until a hedge-line is reached, where to the right by an oak tree you will cross a stile and a plank bridge. Follow the hedge to the right to a stile by a gate near the next corner, with the chimney and tower of Brockhall Hospital directly ahead. In the next field the right-hand hedge leads round to another stile by a gate, beyond which follow the right-hand hedge around two sides of the field. In the first corner you pass close to the ruins of Cravens Farm; in the second corner a stile by a gate leads out of the field and you go forward through another gateway and through the yard of Craven Fold.

Craven Fold to Jumbles Rocks. Join a track on the right enclosed between hedges at the end of the yard, but when the left-hand hedge ends, incline left to a stile beneath a sycamore tree in the far right-hand boundary; then go forward with Brockholes Tower and Pendle ahead. Keep to the right at an isolated barn, which is all that remains of Foggs Farm, beyond which an old track descends to a stile where you enter Great Wood. A worn path continues downhill to a footbridge over Dinckley Brook leading into the grounds of Brockholes Epileptic Hospital. It was originally built as an inebriates' home for 'the reclamation of drunken women' at a time when there were about 85% more drunken females in the county than males.

An enclosed path leads to an access road which you cross, then keep on the right side of a hedge that angles off to reach and cross a stile. Keep alongside the left-hand boundary past a greenhouse and on the outside of a playing field. At the end of this, keep forward along a green track, but leave it when it bends left, as you keep straight on up a slope to cross a stile in a fence. Over the rise aim for a gate on the left of Brockhall Farm buildings. Immediately through this gate turn left through another gate and follow a straight open track to reach the left-hand end of Brockhall Wood. Hurst Green village is prominent on the hill-top ahead across the river, with Stonyhurst College to the right. Bear round to the right as you keep the wood close on your right to reach the riverside near a water-gauge. Just downstream the turbulence is caused by an outcrop in the river bed, called Jumbles Rocks.

Jumbles Rocks to Whalley Abbey. A riverside stile leads into Brockholes Wood where you follow a worn path upstream (continuing after leaving the wood) until you reach the confluence of the Ribble and the Calder, with Hacking Hall standing back to the right. On the opposite bank stands the boat-house from where the Hacking Boat operated, the term given to the old ferry. Also on the far bank are two mounds, said to be the burial place of soldiers killed in the Battle of Billington in 798 A.D. when the Northumbrian armies were raiding. Not far away, at Cross Gills near Hurst Green, is a larger mound surmounted by a cross, where more soldiers are thought to be buried. More recently in 1960, conservationists won a battle against a plan to extract gravel from the river bed.

A dyke leaves the river at this point and leads to a stile on to a track. About 20 yards to the left on the far side of this track, cross another stile and go forward to join the access road coming down to Hacking Hall; follow this road uphill. The track going off on the left is on the line of the Roman road that ran from Ribchester to York, but your way is ahead, to reach a public road where you go left down Pashmire Brow. Bushburn Brook is crossed and you continue along Elker Lane past the old converted Chew Mill, which is said to have made bobbins and clog soles up to about 1911.

Where the road bends sharp right you will see a kissing-gate on the left, through which follow the left-hand boundary. In the next field you have a low bank of trees on your right as you keep ahead to reach the Whalley by-pass by way of a stile on the left side of a railed enclosure. Cross directly to a corresponding stile, then turn left to cross another stile. Now turn your back on the by-pass and follow the right-hand boundary out of a small field and up to the sharp-pointed end of the next field where you cross a stile. Bear left over a narrow field and pass to the right of some allotments to go through a swing gate and along a path leading to a residential road. To the right is the railway viaduct and on the immediate near-side an enclosed path goes off on the left alongside the viaduct and crosses the river Calder at a footbridge. This brings you to a junction.

Those wishing to visit Whalley Abbey remains will find these a short distance to the right beyond the viaduct, and that is also the route for those wishing to terminate the walk at Whalley. It will be noted that the brickwork of the viaduct at this point is ornamental, a small gesture of respect for the abbey ruins.

Whalley Abbey to Edisford Bridge. To continue the walk turn left at the junction along a rough track known as Ridding Lane. After passing beneath the bypass, take the right-hand of two gates; the track passes a sewage works to regain the river bank. Follow it to the right but bear away right after you have crossed a stream, then follow a track uphill. The perimeter railings of Calderstones Mental Hospital confront you; keep them on your right as you join and follow Turkey Lane for over 1 mile to reach Mitton Road. On the opposite side a gate leads into a wood, signposted 'Barraclough'. Keep forward within this narrow wood to the end, then leave the wood by climbing over a rail and cross Barrow Brook at some stepping stones just to the right. Gradually close in on the left-hand boundary, then cross a ditch after passing to the left of a small group of trees. You are now on the line of the Roman road that you crossed earlier and for a short distance your route is along this ancient way. It does not keep alongside the field boundary but bears gradually away and can be traced in places because it is raised slightly from the rest of the field. Confirmation that this is an old route is the base of an old cross further up the field, and this also indicates the spot where you leave the Roman road.

Bear left at the stone base to reach a stile in a corner where the field boundary bends. Keep down the right-hand side of the next two fields to reach a gate leading onto an enclosed strip of land that narrows down to become a track bringing you to Shuttleworth Farm. Go through the yard, turn right and leave at a stile by a gate. Continue past a cottage on your left, and then a farm on the right with the unusual name of Fishes & Peggy Hill. After a short stretch of riverside road the river bends away as you keep forward. Mearley Brook accompanies you for a while, softening the impact of a refuse destruction depot. Ignore a turning on the right and go past Mill House; then enter the wood on the left and walk alongside Mearley Brook, returning to the road to cross the road bridge over the brook and take the turning on the left.

When the way forks, go to the right a few yards to a stile on the left to enter a field. A stile in the far diagonal corner leads onto a riverside path which you follow to reach the picnic site at Edisford Bridge, on the route of the Clitheroe to Preston bus service.

No. 4   BYGONE FERRIES

A circular walk from Edisford Bridge via Mitton 5 miles (optional extension to Calder Foot, total 7½ miles).

Bus to Edisford Bridge.   Maps O.S. 2½" sheets SD 73 and 74.

MITTON has been somewhat isolated for the walker since Hacking Boat ceased to operate but this book would not be complete without its inclusion. Set amid beautiful countryside close to where the Ribble, Hodder and Calder unite, Mitton has the added attraction of a trio of ancient buildings.

Edisford Bridge to Mitton. From the Clitheroe side of the bridge, follow the river downstream through the picnic site and camping ground. After this, the path is enclosed by a wire fence but cross it when you reach a stile. Climb at a slight angle away from the river to a stile on the left of a riverside wood; cross it and go straight across to the corner, then turn left to leave this field at the far diagonal corner. A few yards to the right, turn left down a track to reach a minor road where you go right. Shortly after coming back alongside the river, the road leads past Fishes & Peggy Hill, a house standing back on the left, and reaches Shuttleworth Farm.

Fork right along the riverside track which leads to a water-pipe bridge, where the official right-of-way bears away from the track to by-pass two water-board buildings

No.4

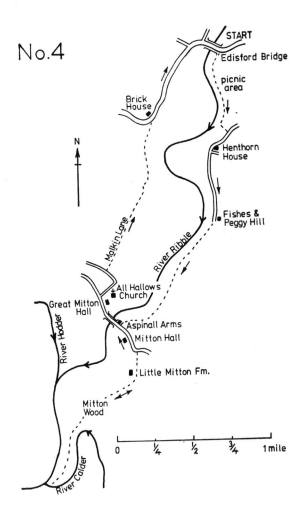

START
Edisford Bridge
picnic area
Brick House
N
Henthorn House
Fishes & Peggy Hill
Malkin Lane
River Ribble
All Hallows Church
Great Mitton Hall
River Hodder
Aspinall Arms
Mitton Hall
Little Mitton Fm.
Mitton Wood
River Calder

0   ¼   ½   ¾   1 mile

and reach a concrete footbridge about 50 yards from the river bank. Climb the rise in the next field to a double stile, then continue along the top of the wooded bank until you cross a treble stile. Bear right to cross through a line of mature trees and join Mitton Road at a stiled gateway on the left-hand side of Aspinalls Arms.

Extension to Calder Foot. Along to the left the road leads past the joint entrance to Mitton Hall and Mitton Hall Farm. Dr. Whitaker, the historian, described the galleried hall in Mitton Hall as one of the finest Gothic rooms he had ever seen in a private house. About 50 yards beyond the entrance, on the same side of the road, look for a gap in the hedge through which, in a belt of trees, is a stile leading into a field.

After crossing a ditch, bear left to pass close to a bend in a fence, then aim to the left-hand side of Little Mitton Farm; enter the field beyond the farm by going through two consecutive gates leading from the yard. Leave by a gate in the far diagonal corner, then cut across a very small corner of the next field to leave at the remains of a stile. Bear left to a line of trees to locate a stile in the boundary fence between the second and third trees.

Go directly over the next field to enter Mitton Wood at a stile in a corner that projects into the field. A faint path that bears left may be traceable but a good guide is to avoid descending prematurely to the river Calder on the left or the river Ribble on the right; at the end of the wood, descend to a stile leading into a field that narrows to a point at the confluence of the two rivers. At one time the journey could have been continued by Hacking Boat either across the Calder to Hacking Hall or across the Ribble; for lack of a replacement the route back to Mitton has to be retraced. An angler's track leads back via the Ribble (past Hodder Foot) and the yard of Mitton Hall Farm, but it is not clear whether this is a right-of-way.

Mitton to Edisford Bridge. Having returned to Mitton Road, turn left to cross Mitton bridge and climb up to Great Mitton Hall and All Hallows church. The nave of the church is said to date from 1270 and the tower from the 15th century. Of great interest is the chapel built in 1594 by Sir Richard Sherbourne (Shireburne) of Stonyhurst. Originally the highway passed to the other side of the church and hall and led down to Mitton Boat, another bygone ferry.

Church Lane is on the right at the top of the hill and it leads past the school. On the right, after a bend, are Poultry Farm Cottages, then a gated access road. Go through the wide gateway on the right with stone gateposts nearly opposite Bailey Cottages; turn left along the hedge which bears right and disappears. You are now walking alongside a sunken overgrown green track (Malkin Lane). Continue beside it past a new farm building. The right-of-way is still beside the lane but you may find the lane itself easier going from this point on. Cross a barbed wire fence; then, when you come to a gate in the left-hand boundary of the lane, enter the field on the left and continue alongside the green lane.

Before reaching the corner, bear left to cross a rail midway between the lane and a small wood on the left. A few yards ahead, cross a bridged stream and then follow it until it bends right. Keep forward here to cross a barbed-wire fence (no stile at the time of writing), then continue forward to join and follow another stream. Cross a rail at the end of the field and keep alongside the stream to cross a sheep wire fence. Carry on to a sleeper bridge which takes you across the stream; a gate at the end of the field gives access to a track that leads to the road opposite to Brick House. Edisford Bridge is over $\frac{1}{2}$ mile to the right.

No. 5   **YES, THIS IS LANCASHIRE**

A circular walk from De Tabley Arms (near Ribchester) via Dinckley Bridge 4½ miles (alternatively, finish at Hurst Green 3 miles).

Bus to De Tabley Arms.   Map O.S. 2½″ sheet SD 63.

"I HAVE chosen this area to settle down in — here, in my opinion is typical English landscape at its best." These words spoken by a non-Lancastrian who has travelled all over the country are perhaps the best introduction to a walk in the area to which he refers.

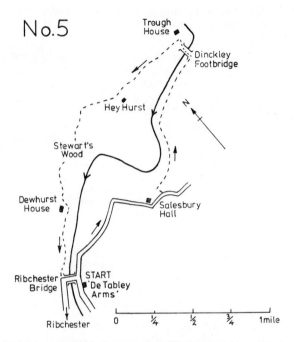

No.5

Trough House

Dinckley Footbridge

Hey Hurst

N

Stewart's Wood

Dewhurst House

Salesbury Hall

Ribchester Bridge

START 'De Tabley Arms'

Ribchester

0   ¼   ½   ¾   1mile

De Tabley Arms to Dinckley Bridge. Follow the route as described in walk No. 3 until you reach Dinckley suspension bridge; this was erected in 1951 as a replacement for the ferry which was operated from Trough House, the farm across the river. The original ferry boats were called trows; they resembled a couple of cattle troughs fastened together abreast and punted across the river with a pole. The name of the farm is a reminder of the old craft.

Dinckley Bridge to De Tabley Arms. Cross the bridge and follow the right-hand fence almost to the yard of Trough House. If you wish to finish at Hurst Green, pass through the yard and follow the farm road which climbs most of the way, to reach the village after one mile.

For the circular walk, do not enter the yard but turn sharp left along a rutted track that goes uphill and diagonally back towards the river at first, then keep to the right-hand fence. Choose the right-hand gateway in the field corner, then turn left to follow the left-hand boundary through three fields to reach a footbridge over Starling Brook on the left of Clough Bank Wood.

Over the bridge, follow the right-hand boundary up and around two sides of a field to join the access road above Hey Hurst at a rail tucked into the top corner. Climb the stile almost opposite on the other side of the road, then cross the next field to an oak tree which stands in the far bottom corner; ignore a stile beside a white gate only a matter of yards to the left of the oak tree. Cross the rail on the right of the oak tree and follow the left-hand fence until it bends left downhill. Bear right here, gradually climbing; over to your right a fence will come into view whilst on the left front Hough Wood slopes down to the river. Close to the right-hand side of the wood is a footbridge, almost invisible until you reach it. Over this keep forward to cross another footbridge, then continue alongside the left-hand iron rail fence.

Cut across a bend in the wood boundary, then descend to pass through a small gate in a hollow; climb the slope ahead and pass alongside the right-hand side of Stewart's Wood. At the end of the wood there is an iron rail to climb (alternatively use the gate 50 yards to the right); then keep forward, with a fence over to your right. Pass the top end of two tree-lined gullies that head downhill towards the river, and turn diagonally downhill to the far left-hand corner of the field to join an old sunken tunnel-like track beneath the trees. This goes down to Dewhurst House where a gate leads into the yard (a sea of mud and muck may cause you to seek an alternative way into the yard). Follow the farm road to the right to reach the Blackburn road at Ribchester Bridge. De Tabley Arms is across the river.

A circular walk from Hurst Green, via Hacking Boat House. 7¼ miles.

Bus to Hurst Green.   Maps O.S. 2½″ sheets SD 63 and 73.

FROM the word go, this walk is in the heart of Ribble Valley walking country, including a true riverside walk that goes by the confluences of the Calder and Hodder with the Ribble.   Lonely and derelict, Hacking Boat House stands as a monument to the old ferry; a replacement would greatly enhance the amenities of the Ribble Valley.

Hurst Green to Hacking Boat House. Leave the road by going down the Clitheroe side of the Shireburn Arms. A left-hand wall leads to a stiled gateway, beyond which follow the right-hand hedge downhill, with Billington Moor ahead across the Ribble Valley and Pendle Hill to the left. After passing Parker's Well, the hedge swings away and you bear right, over a depression, to regain the hedge further on.   Locate a footbridge beneath the trees at the bottom of the field, then go forward over another footbridge and follow the left-hand boundary of Raid Deep Wood.   Enter the wood at a stile to the right of the field corner and follow a worn path downhill through the wood to a footbridge leading into a field.   This is the start of the riverside walk; go towards the pipe-bridge.

After nearly 1 mile, which involves crossing a number of stiles, a track comes alongside the river and leads to Jumbles Farm.   Fork right there to regain the river-bank at Jumbles Rocks, an outcrop in the river bed.   This is the site of Bullasey Ford that dated from Roman times and was on the old road to Stonyhurst; you may have noticed a related outcrop of rock a little way downstream.   After going through a stiled gateway at the end of the next field, head for the right-hand side of Hacking Boat House, then head back gradually to the river at the confluence with the Calder, with Hacking Hall on the far bank.

Behind the Boat House, to the north and north-east, are two mounds, thought to be the burial places of warriors

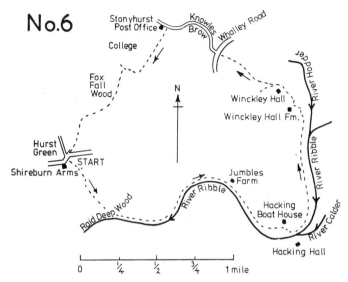

No.6

Stonyhurst Post Office

College

Knowles Brow

Whalley Road

River Hodder

Fox Fall Wood

N

Winckley Hall

Winckley Hall Fm.

Hurst Green

START

Shireburn Arms

River Ribble

Jumbles Farm

River Ribble

Hacking Boat House

River Calder

Road Deep Wood

Hacking Hall

0   ¼   ½   ¾   1 mile

killed at the battle of Billington (Billangahoh) in 798, when Eardulph the Northumbrian beat Wadda the Saxon Chieftain. Relics of the battle have now been unearthed, including a rude stone coffin found in 1836, containing human bones and warlike implements.

Hacking Boat House to Whalley Road. A characteristic of the next stretch in July is the white patches of crowfoot scattered like stepping-stones across the river.

The confluence of the Hodder and Ribble is ¾ mile further on and an enclosed track begins here, with a splendid oak on the left near the start. A section of the track, which leads to Winckley Hall Farm (formerly Winckley Hall), is bordered by an iron chain, a reminder that a former tenant was a colliery owner, for the chain was used to pull trucks, some of which have been used as water-troughs on the farm.

Bear left and right in the yard to join the farm road that leads uphill. Keep to the main route which goes by the new Winckley Hall (now a private nursing home) standing back in the trees on the left. When the way levels out and bends left, go through an iron kissing-gate on the right

29

next to a field gate. Cross the field to a similar gate, beyond which you see Kemple End (the steep shoulder of Longridge Fell) ahead, with Stonyhurst College on the left front. Aim to come alongside Spring Wood on the right; then, when you reach the end of it, keep forward downhill and through two fields to Whalley Road.

Whalley Road to Hurst Green. Cross straight over and continue up Knowles Brow until you turn off along a minor road on the left, on the nearside of Stonyhurst post office. Ignore a right fork near the start, and at a junction of track keep straight on, with a red-brick wall on the right, to enter a field. Go alongside a stone building on your left to a kissing-gate in the corner to reach another junction. Turn right. After a straight stretch, when the road bends right, go through a gate in the corner on the left. Keep at first to the left-hand side of a long narrow field, then cross over to continue alongside Fox Fall Wood. Descend to cross a stream and then climb to pass through a kissing-gate.   Keep the hedge on the right and pass through the next kissing-gate after this, but by-pass a third kissing-gate as you bear left around the field to leave at a fourth kissing-gate in the next corner. Cut across a small corner of the next field, then follow the right-hand stone wall before joining a track that leads to Hurst Green.

No. 7   **IN A NUTSHELL**

A circular walk from Beacon Hostel, Longridge, via Dilworth Bottoms.   **4¼ miles.**

Bus to Beacon Hostel. (N.B. : Week-end service almost non-existent; the alternative is to alight at the White Bull, Longridge). Map O.S. 2½" sheet SD 63.

BEAUTIFUL countryside, excellent views and a string of interesting places and items; it is hard to believe that so much can be contained in such a short walk.

Beacon Hostel to Written Stone. If you have alighted at the White Bull, fork left at the hotel along Higher Road for one-third of a mile to reach Beacon Hostel, a building now converted into flats. Originally it was the Crown Hotel (the name, although painted over, can still be seen) and later a Youth Hostel, hence the name of the bus terminus. Just beyond is the Berries Restaurant which was at one time a public house called, significantly, Quarrymans Arms, later to become Cottage Cafe.

Leave Higher Road by turning down the metalled road on the nearside and adjacent to Berries Restaurant; this is Tan Yard Lane and it bends left at Fern Cottage, then right, downhill. Leave the lane at this second bend as you keep forward over a stiled gateway along a track that leads to a flooded quarry, with Beacon View caravan site over on the left. It was from this spot that the stone was taken to build Preston Municipal Buildings; Longridge stone was also used for Preston's Free Library. The stone was first quarried extensively in 1830, some of it being taken by horse and cart to Liverpool for building the docks. In 1840 the Preston-Longridge railway was opened for the purpose of developing the stone trade. Horses pulled the empty trucks uphill to the quarries, but were able to ride in railway vans on the return journey as the loaded trucks rumbled down the gradient. It was due to the stone trade that Longridge grew faster than neighbouring places such as Goosnargh, Chipping and Ribchester, but high railway charges eventually ended this prosperity. The area of the quarries is called Tootle Height, a name thought to mean "watch" or "look-out hill"; despite the onslaught of the quarrymen, the area still commands extensive views.

The way bends right at the quarry, then ends with a tennis court on the right. Turn your back to the tennis court and go forward over some rough ground and through some trees and shrubs; then, after a few yards look for a less conspicuous fork to the right, with sight of a concrete post and wire-netting fence to the left. This right fork leads to an iron rail-stile in the fence in about 16 yards, leading on to a track enclosed between a wall and a fence. Go left along this path which bears right and crosses a stone stile (ignore the nearby stile on the right), then shortly after continues between two wire fences to reach an open space. This is the parking area of Blackpool and Fylde Kart Club.

Cross the open space and go to the left of a barn that has been converted into toilets, then follow a track past a modernised cottage (behind the converted barn) to reach another open space and a rough extension of the kart track. Go forward to the fenceless field and cross this, bearing left from the line of overhead electricity wires to a flight of well-worn stone steps that climb the far boundary wall, atop of which is a track — Written Stone Lane. Despite alterations that take place occasionally to the area just passed through, the line of the footpath remains constant; difficulties of any kind should be reported. (N.B. There is an additional right-of-way that passes to the right of the converted barn and cottage, and then links up with the route already described.)

Go right alongside the wall for about 70 yards to where the way forks. To the left is the old farmhouse of Green Banks and the old Copy Quarry which was re-opened to extract stone for the Broughton-Blackpool motorway and has since been landscaped. Your way is ahead through a gap-stile in the stone wall-cum-gatepost along Written Stone Lane, now a grassy track between two stone walls. It narrows down and is often water-logged but is easy to follow, bringing you to a farm road near Written Stone Farm.

Your way is to the left but, if you wish to see the stone which gives the farm and lane their name, go forward a few yards to a junction — the stone is on your right. There are many stories about the stone, which incidentally stands on the line of the Roman road that went from Ribchester to Lancaster. It is thought to have been placed here by one of the Radcliffes, following four deaths in the family within a short space of time. At a later date, one of the farm tenants moved it to use as a buttery-stone, but was constantly plagued by the antics of objects placed on it, which tilted over and clattered about during the night. Another story tells of the stone being erected in a nearby field as a rubbing stone for the cattle, which event was followed by a succession of misfortunes to the farmer concerned; in both cases, when the stone was replaced, peace was restored.

Written Stone to the White Bull. Retrace your steps to where you joined the farm road and continue along it to reach Cottam House Farm. Cottam Hall, also known as Knoll Hall, stood here and was the home of the Cottams, who with the Radcliffes were two of the influential old families of the district. Continue through the spacious yard to join a grassy track, which you follow downhill to reach the Hurst Green road at a gate. Cross the road to a

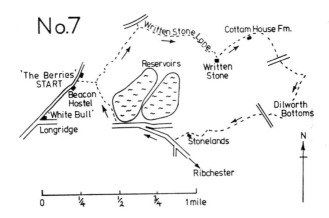

Written Stone Lane

Cottam House Fm.

Reservoirs

Written
Stone

'The Berries'
START

Beacon
Hostel

'White Bull'

Longridge

Dilworth
Bottoms

Stonelands

Ribchester

N

| 0 | ¼ | ½ | ¾ | 1 mile |

stile a few yards to your right by a bus shelter, signposted
"Dilworth Bottoms." Follow the left-hand hedge to a stile
in the field corner, over which follow the left-hand wall and
hedge to cross a wall-stile. Now follow the line of a shallow depression and bear slightly left downhill, to join an
enclosed woodside path at a stile. If there has been plenty
of rain, it is worthwhile going left a short distance to a
footbridge to view Cowley Brook as it flows through White
Carr Wood. This brook once provided the power to run
seven mills.

Your way is downstream, along the banktop with the
brook on your left. Keep a look-out for a flight of stone
steps on the left which will take you down to join a road at
the ruins of the old smithy. Go left along this road, passing Woodbine Cottage and Springs Farm and cottages, to
reach a ford at Dilworth Bottoms, with a spring dated
"D.B. 1861" in the banking on your right. Do not cross
the ford but continue with the brook on your left to reach
a second ford, where the road re-crosses the brook. There
is also a footbridge over the brook, but do not cross this.
Instead, go through the gate on your right on the nearside
of a wooden garage and incline left uphill, over a bumpy
field and then along a left-hand hedge. Cross this at a stile
as you start to drop down to Page Brook and follow a left-
hand hedge to Ward Green Lane, reached by passing between the hedge and a cabin (route somewhat difficult at
the time of writing).

Go right along the lane to a gate on the left after 50 yards, through which you follow the left-hand hedge to a gate in the field corner. Keep forward in the next field along the highest ground to reach a stile at a gateway in an extended part of the field. Bear slightly right after this, along the line of a shallow depression, to cross a double stile on the right of a pond. Go left along the left-hand fence, before bearing right in a narrow end of the field, to leave by a gate in the right-hand corner. Continue along the left-hand hedge, then bear right to a gate that takes you into the yard of Stoneland. Go left after passing the rear of the house, then turn right along the farm road to reach Blackburn Road at Elm House. Go right then left to pass the Corporation Arms, then leave the road immediately after passing the reservoir on the right, by turning up Tan Yard Lane. This leads uphill to reach a "T" junction after passing a modern bungalow; go left here to reach Higher Road.

No. 8   A ROAMIN' WITH THE ROMANS

A circular walk from Alston via Ribchester.   8½ miles. (Can be done as two separate rambles — Alston to Ribchester or vice versa).

Bus: The stop after the White Bull, Alston.   Map O.S. 2½" sheet SD 63.

A FACT that is perhaps not readily appreciated is that the Romans were stationed at Ribchester for three hundred years. Their soldiers marched along the roads that radiated from the fortress town and, in a more casual manner, they moved around the local countryside. It would be a different landscape then, wild and wooded, but even so there is something exciting to be "A roamin' with the Romans."

Alston to Lord's Farm. From the bus-stop beyond the White Bull, walk back about 50 yards to an access road that goes off on the opposite side of the road, signposted "Bridleway." This is Pinfold Lane and in the corner of the field on the right, at the start of the lane, is the base of an old wayside cross. When the way forks, keep alongside the embankment of Alston reservoir No. 3, then fork right at the end of the reservoir. When the road bends right, go through a kissing-gate on the left and continue with Alston reservoir No. 1 over on your left.

Cross a rail to enter the next field and go past a pond that is on your right, then follow a right-hand hedge which bends away to cross the top end of a gully. Bear away after this, aiming for the far left-hand corner, where you will find a footbridge in a hollow. As you climb the bank after crossing the bridge, bear right (with red-bricked Welch House Farm on your right front). Hidden in a gully ahead is a footbridge (look for a Ramblers' Association waymark — an arrow on a tree) and over this you climb up to reach Hothersall Lane at a stile.

Continue by the farm road opposite, then cross a stile and pass between a fence and barn. A short way down the field, cross a stile in the left-hand boundary, signified by a Ramblers' Association signpost, then aim for the older barns across the field, to join an access road at a gate. Enter the yard of Butcher Fold opposite, then bear right and left to leave the yard on the north-east side at a gate that leads into a field. Follow the left-hand hedge to cross a stile tucked into a corner, then choose the right-hand of two more stiles. Keep the same direction to cross a fence ahead with a water-trough on your left, after which you will reach a fenced-off depression. Skirt around to the right until a stile in the fence leads on to a grass track which curves down to cross a brook (culverted at crossing point) and then climbs to go by Hades Farm and continues to join a minor road; along to the right is a farm road on the left that leads towards Lord's Farm.

Lord's Farm to Ribchester. Fork to the right-hand side of the farmhouse and follow the track until it ends beyond an isolated barn. Pass through the left-hand gateway and aim to the left of a small circular copse, to leave the field in the far left-hand corner. On the immediate left, another gateway leads onto an enclosed tract of land clothed with trees and bushes which you follow to the right. Some way after crossing a stile, join a track that comes in from the left and leads through a gateway ahead. Keep forward over an open area that offers good views, the most prominent landmark being Ribblesdale Mill chimney at Ribchester, on your left front.

35

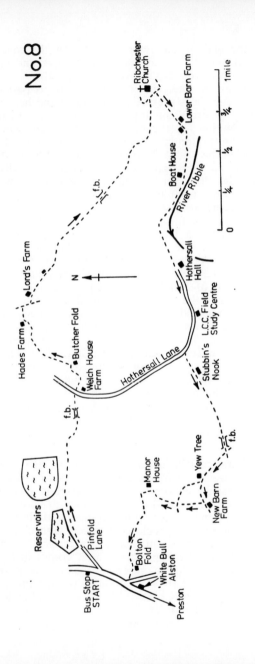

No.8

The land falls to a footbridge at the confluence of two streams, over which bear slightly left, uphill, to cross a stiled gateway near a corner in the boundary ahead. There is a hedge on the right to follow at first; then after passing a pond, keep the same direction, gradually descending, with Ribchester church on your left front. Beyond a stile in a fence, join the right-hand hedge which will bring you round to join a track at a stiled gateway. You can follow the track all the way into Ribchester; alternatively, at the second left bend there is a stile on the right, from where you can go alongside the churchyard wall to reach the riverside and the Roman Museum. Very little trace is left of the Roman occupation, but for those who wish to delve into the past there are books that will turn this Lancashire village into a source of wonder.

Ribchester to Hothersall Hall. As you go alongside the churchyard wall to reach the riverside, you will pass by a small gate leading into the yard; for those wishing to return to Alston, this can be the starting point. Turn your back on the gate and walk away from the church to cross a stile in the field corner, then cross a stile on the opposite side of an access road. Beyond a stile at the end of the next field, aim towards Lower Barn Farm to cross a footbridge, then join the farm road by a gate on the left. Across the river is Osbaldeston Hall, for several centuries up until the mid-eighteenth century the seat of the Osbaldeston family; most of the present house is thought to be early 17th century. The Osbaldestons owned a ferry across the river, which is recorded as long ago as 1355.

Follow the road to the right, past Lower Barn Farm and on to Boat House, a reminder of the ferry. Two fields after this the track fades away and the route is alongside a riverside boundary. On leaving this field, climb a hillside by way of a green track that bends round to reach the top of the wooded riverside bank. Leave the track here, to keep to the wood side at first, but instead of descending to the river, keep forward along the rough hillside; then descend to join a track at a gate, which leads to Hothersall Hall to the left. Worthy of note before reaching the farm is a large ornamental water-trough cut out of a single piece of stone and dated 1882. The Hothersall family appear to have been connected with this estate for 600 years. The present hall was rebuilt in the last century by Jonathan Openshaw, a prosperous woollen manufacturer from Bury.

Hothersall Hall to Alston. After passing the house, fork right uphill and continue past the Lancashire County Field Study Centre, formerly a boys' camp. Woodlands Farm signals the start of another climb which brings you to a turning on the left after passing a bungalow called Greenacres. This turning leads to Stubbins Nook, a fine example of a Lancashire "longhouse" built completely of dressed stone; the pillars in the garden were rescued from an Accrington mill. Keep forward beyond the house, along the right-hand side of three fields, descending to cross a footbridge on the left-hand side of King Wood.

Climb directly from the bridge to cross the next hedge-line at a stile, then bear right to a gate in the far top corner of the field; beyond the gate an enclosed track leads to the red-bricked Yew Tree house. Keep left here, then continue straight on towards New Barn Farm. Before reaching the farmhouse, go through a gate on the right on the nearside of a corrugated shippon and cross the hedge behind at a rail (no stile at time of writing). Go forward in line with two trees, then bear slightly right to cross a fence (no stile at time of writing). Keep forward to join Thorn Lane at a stiled gateway and continue, after crossing a cattle grid, along the concrete road that lies ahead.

This leads to Manor House, but turn left after crossing another cattle grid, along a green track, which you leave when it bends right by passing through a gap-stile on the left. In the next corner, cross a stile, then bear right to cross a stile and plank at the corner of the hedge that comes in from the left. Follow the right-hand hedge until it bends away, then keep straight ahead to join a farm track; turn left along this. The track becomes enclosed and weaves its way between the buildings of Bolton Croft to reach the main road near the White Bull; you may have to use your ingenuity to avoid the slurry on this last section!

**A circular walk from Salesbury via Whalley Nab.
12 miles.**

**(Can be treated as two separate rambles — Salesbury to
Billington 6½ miles; Billington to Salesbury 5½ miles).**

*Bus to Bonny Inn, Salesbury, via Ribchester. If only
half the walk is done the journey to or from Billington by
bus will have to be via Blackburn.   The bus stop at Billington is at the Band Club, or alternatively ask for Judge
Walmsley; nearby is the road to York, which you take to
start the second half of the ramble. Maps O.S. 2½" sheets
SD 63 and 73.*

FROM an elevated start, the route gradually descends
towards the union of the Ribble and Calder valleys, giving
an ever-changing view of this beautiful area. Here is a
greenness typical of England and especially of Lancashire,
which impresses visitors from overseas although we some-
times take it for granted.   The character of the walk
changes as the route climbs Whalley Nab and Billington
Moor, where the views become more extensive.

Salesbury to Old Langho.   Just beyond the bus shelter at
Bonny Inn, an opening between the houses leads into Lovely
Hall Lane opposite St. Peter's church; cross over and go
down the enclosed footpath between the church and the
large graveyard. On reaching the field at the end, cross
the stile on the left and go down the side of the cricket field
alongside the graveyard.   Continue round the bottom end
of the field until you come to where a path angles down
the bank on your left to a stile.   After going down the left
side of the next field, follow a track to the left to reach
Ashes Farm.   Immediately you have left the yard turn
right, across a wild and watery piece of land to reach a
stile.   Over this, the remains of an old track crosses the
site of a demolished building and goes over a rise.   Now
follow a line of mature trees downhill, with Lovely Hall
over on your left.

Bear left at the end of the line of trees, towards the
houses of Copster Green at the top of a hillside.   Cross a
plank-bridge and stile at the foot of the hill, then keep the
same direction to reach a stile in the right-hand boundary.
Over this, across a narrow field is another stile, after which

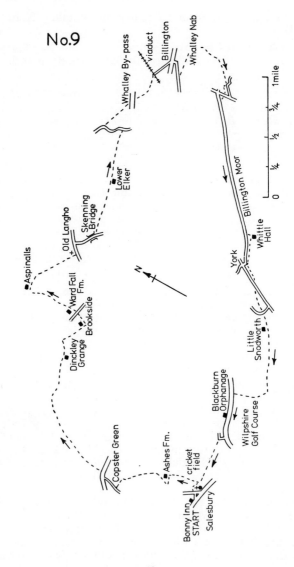

No.9

Whalley By-pass
viaduct
Billington
Whalley Nab
Lower Elker
Skenning Bridge
Old Langho
Aspinalls
Ward Fall Fm.
Brookside
Dinckley Grange
Copster Green
Ashes Fm.
cricket field
Bonny Inn
START
Salesbury
Blackburn Orphanage
Wilpshire Golf Course
Little Snodworth
York
Whittle Hall
Billington Moor

N

0   ¼   ½   ¾   1mile

your way is uphill to your left to reach the green at Copster.

Longsight Road is to your right, across which is Park Gate Inn, a name that reminds us of the days when the Talbots of Salesbury Hall owned an estate stretching down to the river. For this walk, turn right along the main road, then turn up the farm road on the far side just around the first bend, signposted "Tanners Arms, Dinckley." This takes you between Copster Hall Farm (built 1615) and Copster Hall Bungalow. Beyond a cattle grid keep forward alongside the right-hand boundary (avoiding an inviting gateway) to enter the next field, with an isolated barn to your right.

At the bottom of the next field the right-hand hedge bends, bringing you to a gateway leading into a sloping field. Bear left down this to reach Park Brook, which is crossed at a footbridge close to the left-hand fence. Climb up alongside the left-hand boundary through the next two fields, continuing in the second field until you reach a double stile in the second corner. Over this you have a wooden fence over on your left as you head for Dinckley Grange Farm. After passing between two oak trees, aim to the left of the farm to join the farm road leading from the yard. When the road bends left, cross the stile standing back on the right; then follow the right-hand fence/hedge at first, but bear away to enter the next field at a cart platform utilised as a bridge. Bear left to join and follow the left-hand hedge which descends to Brook Side Cottage, reached by climbing over a wire fence.

Pass between the cottage and Dinckley Brook, then just before you reach the end of the next field, bear away from the brook and cross a stile. Cross another field to join a road by a stile to the left of a gate. Almost opposite this a road leads up to Ward Fall, an 18th century building whose surroundings have been attractively landscaped. Enter the field beyond at a small gate in a wooden fence and make towards Aspinalls, the farmhouse ahead. Prominent on your right front are the water-tower and chimney at Brockhall Hospital, half right is Pendle Hill, and Whalley Nab with its television relay mast is to your right.

When a fence is met in a fold of the land, you will find a stile near the left-hand line of trees. Still heading for Aspinalls, look for a stile concealed by the right-hand one

41

of a pair of old sheds; then bear slightly left across the narrow part of an uneven field to a stile. Over this, go alongside a right-hand hedge to a gate on the right beyond a stone barn. Once through the gate turn left to join the farm road. This is on the line of the Roman road that ran from Ribchester to York and two stones discovered here are evidence of this; one, a conical-shaped edging stone is in Ribchester Museum, the other (rutted by wear) is built into the old stables.

Turn right along the farm road to pass the old stables and Aspinalls farmhouse (formerly called Tan Pits) and continue along a short length of grass track. After a gateway, bear right across a field to pass close to the end of a hedge coming in from your left; the ground suddenly falls away at this point and you drop down alongside a line of small trees on your left to a footbridge across Dinckley Brook. Over this, climb a slope and then join the left-hand hedge that leads towards the black and white Black Bull Hotel at Old Langho; a stile in the field corner leads onto a grass track to reach the road.

Old Langho to Billington. On your left is old St. Leonard's church, built in 1557 — some of the stones came from Whalley Abbey — where services are held once a month. After passing the church, turn right at Keepers Cottage (post office and store) along Northcote Road. Leemings Farm is passed, then Bushburn Brook is crossed at Skenning Bridge. Go through the gate on the left after this and straight across (with Pendle on your left front) to a double stile in a short length of wooden fencing. Cut across a corner of the next field as you bear right to join and follow the right-hand hedge. Cross a track and keep the same direction to leave the field by a stile beneath an oak tree near the top right-hand corner. Descend to cross a footbridge, then cross a stile to your left. Follow a shallow depression that starts here, but when you reach a left-hand hedge, bear right to a railed gateway leading onto a grass track which brings you to Lower Elker.

Enter the muddy yard after passing a barn on your right, then join a track that leaves on your left. This descends to cross a tributary of Bushburn Brook by a small wooden bungalow. Leave the track here to climb a low bank, then follow a faint trail that rejoins the track where it is gated, with Whalley railway viaduct ahead. Just beyond the gate turn left along a road which bends left, right and left again. Enter the field on the right at this last bend by means of a kissing-gate and follow a left-hand fence. In the next field keep forward to reach the Whalley by-pass road with the river Calder close on your left. A stile on the left-hand side of a small enclosure leads onto the road with a corresponding stile on the other side. Cross the stile to your left, then follow an iron fence away from the by-pass to leave this small triangular enclosure by a stile in a sharp-pointed corner. Follow the right-hand hedge to another stile in the top corner, then bear left and go past some allotments to a kissing-gate that leads by way of a second kissing-gate to Sunnyside Avenue. Turn right then join the road that goes beneath the viaduct (built 1850 — 53 arches) to reach the main road at Billington.

Billington to York. Just to the right on the far side of the road is the road that leads to York (Lancashire). It makes a sharp bend, then goes past four rows of attractive cottages at Painter Wood (two rows on either side). After the last cottage of the second row on the left, a track doubles back through a gate; there is a stile down to the right. A foretaste of the views to come can be had from this track as you follow it up to join the road that has climbed steeply from Whalley Bridge. A farm track on the opposite side of the road, sign-posted "Private Road, footpath only," continues the route. Take a well-earned rest when you come to a seat and enjoy the views off Whalley Nab, with Pendle Hill a dominant feature across the Calder valley.

When you reach a wooded section on the right at a cattle grid, leave the road and go up the right-hand fringe of the wood until you see a stile up the steeper slope on your left. At the top of the slope join the left-hand boundary wall of the wood, with new views opening up. After a small open area a stile leads to the left-hand side of Higher Whalley Banks Farm (in the process of re-building). Look for a stile in the wall on the right on the nearside of a small outbuilding; this leads onto a track which, after nearly $\frac{1}{4}$ mile, brings you to Hawcliffe Lane. Leave the lane at once by turning up an enclosed track on your right, but after a few yards cross a stile on the left. Skirt round a sparsely wooded slope on your right to reach another road, which you cross by two corresponding stiles. Now follow the right-hand boundary to reach Moor Lane with Nab Top Farm close to your left, the direction you have to take.

The next section of the walk is along the top of Billington Moor and entails walking along the road, but fortunately Moor Lane is a quiet and scenic route. After 1¼ miles, when you have just climbed a slight rise, you will see York village about ¼ mile ahead. Leave the road at this point by turning up a track on the left which brings you to Whittle Hill Farm. Enter the yard on the right, then go round to the left to cross a stile. Go to the right, with a long building on your right, and alongside the boundary wall of a wood. Keep forward beyond a stile to reach another stile that leads onto the road at York.

York to Salesbury. Do not join the road here but keep on along the lower slope of a gorse-strewn hillside, following a faint path that gradually closes in on the road on the right, before joining it after nearly ¼ mile at a stile by a gate. Go a few yards to the left, then cross another stile by a gate on the far side of the road. Bear left and pass over a small hillock (Fish Moor) to join a left-hand fence that leads you to Snodworth Road. On the opposite side a farm road leads down to Little Snodworth Farm. After passing straight through and out of the yard, go a few yards alongside the lefthand wall, then cross it at a stile, to continue with the wall on your right; you are now on Wilpshire Moor. Keep the same direction when the wall ends, now following a low ridge. Bear slightly left when you reach the end of the ridge, as you climb up to the top of a rise from where Wilpshire Golf Course comes into view and is entered by a wooden stile in the stone boundary wall. Turn downhill and join the fence that comes in from the right, then keep down the right-hand side of the course. Bear left a little at the bottom to enter a rough piece of ground between house gardens and reach Whalley New Road.

Cross over and go to your left past Blackburn orphanage, then part-way round a bend in the road until you are opposite the gates of White Lodge. Turn down the estate road on the right here, but before reaching the bottom of the hill, cross over the rough ground on your left to join an enclosed path at a stile. Make sure that you follow this path to the very end where a stile leads into a field (ignore the stile and kissing-gate half-way along). Bear slightly right in the next field to a stile on to a track, which you cross directly, to enter a modern estate. After passing a dormer bungalow follow the estate road that goes forward and crosses another road. At the end, join a path enclosed between high garden fences that leads into a field, on the far side of which is the enclosed path on the right of St. Peter's church where you started the walk.

No. 10   SURVEY THE VALLEY

A circular walk from the Windmill Hotel, Mellor, via Salesbury.   **9 miles.**
(For those who are not dependent upon public transport, this walk can be started and finished at the Fieldens Arms, Mellor Brook, reducing the route to 8 miles).
Bus to Windmill Hotel, Mellor. Map O.S. 2½" sheet SD 63.

THE SCOPE for walking in the Ribble Valley seems limitless; this route is but one instance. Towards the end of the walk a superb view of the valley, and much further afield, can be seen from Mellor Moor. It is encouraging in this area to find many well-worn paths, indicating that the local people make good use of them.

Windmill Hotel to Mire Fold. The hotel stands at the junction of Blackburn New Road and Branch Road. The latter leads down to the Whalley road at Mellor Brook opposite the Fieldens Arms; here the two routes join. Go along in the Whalley direction for about 50 yards, then turn down Higher Commons Lane on the left. This descends to cross Mellor Brook, then passes through a narrow neck of Mammon Wood and bends right. Look for a stile on the left and go directly across a field to the far boundary. Turn right (keeping inside the same field) and follow the hedge to a stile in the corner after passing a pit. Cross the stile and go forward (passing to the right of a tree-lined pond) to a stile on the left of another pit. Keep forward down the left-hand side of the next two fields to Commons Lane.

A stile on the opposite side of the road is crossed, then keep forward to cross a footbridge at the far boundary.

Continue down the left-hand side of four fields (small, large, small, large), to leave the fourth at a stile in the corner. Turn right and go round two sides of the next irregular field to the corner. Step over the fence (no stile at time of writing) and cross the footbridge into the following field. Close to your left is the site of Sandiford Well, but your way is alongside the right-hand hedge through two fields, divided by a wire fence; keep forward in the next field to join a minor road at a stile by a gate.

Follow this road to the right and ignore turnings on the right and left as you keep on past Park Gate and Little Oxendale. When the road bends left through Oxendale Hall gateway, your way is forward along an enclosed grass track sign-posted "Longsight Road." This track leads to Mire Wood where it becomes a narrow worn path going down to a stream, which has to be forded. Climb the opposite bank to a sunken path about 10 yards from the stream. Turn right along this (ignoring the "path" which seems to go straight ahead), and after five or six yards follow it round to the left and uphill, passing a mossy tree-stump on your left. Soon you should come to a rail stile in a wire fence by a tree, with a gate about 60 yards away to the left. If you miss the stile do not try to climb the gate or the fence — follow the fence till you come to the stile, which is quite unmistakable.

Beyond this fence the trees are spaced wider apart and shortly after this you leave the wood. Still keeping forward up rising ground, pass to the right of a depression and through a line of trees. When Mire Fold Farm comes into view, aim to the left of the buildings (a worn cow-trail shows the way) to reach the far right-hand corner of the field, where a narrow neck of the field leads via a stile to a junction with the farm road. A land-mine fell in this vicinity during the last war, causing damage to Mire Fold barn which had to be buttressed; damage was also done to nearby Showley Hall.

Mire Fold to Salesbury. Turn left, away from the farm through a gate; then go along a green track to reach a winding narrow road, which you follow to the right for over $\frac{1}{2}$ mile to join Ribchester Road. Keep forward along this road for nearly 200 yards, to a gate on the left at the start of the garden wall of White Holme. Through this gate, follow the curve of the garden fence to a gateway in the field corner, then cross the next field, passing by a lone oak tree.

Enter the right-hand field that lies ahead; then, after skirting round a pond, keep to the left-hand hedge and leave the field by a stile in the corner. Bear right to reach the far boundary which you follow in the direction of the main road. Your way descends into a hollow, where a concealed stile on the left leads onto a track which goes by Mill House, crosses Park Brook and goes up to join the main road.

Cross over and continue up Lovely Hall Lane. After the last house on the right, leave the road by a footpath

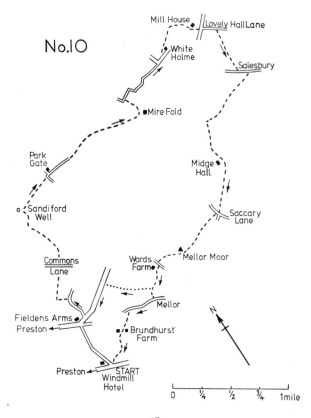

on the right, signposted "Ribchester Road." There is a stone wall on the left at first, then an enclosed section, after which keep to the left-hand boundary. When the hedge bends away, keep straight on uphill to reach Ribchester Road at Salesbury by way of a tract of land between house gardens.

Salesbury to Mellor Moor. Go to the left for 150 yards, then turn down a track on the right alongside a stone wall. Beyond a stile the track gradually descends and then passes under some high-tension wires. Shortly after this the track bears away from the left-hand hedge and heads for a gate, where you cross a stile. After about 40 yards a farm road comes in from the left; turn left down this road to cross Showley Brook. Go past Beverley Kennels (factory house) and up to Midge Hall Farm.

Go straight past the farmhouse to a stile at the end of the yard. Beyond this the way becomes a worn, narrow path, but leave it when you are opposite a small brick structure and bear right, uphill, to a double stile in the hedge coming up from the right. Go over the stile and straight across the field to a stile and plank bridge in a hollow, beyond which you follow the right-hand hedge over a small rise. Pass through a gap and over another plank bridge on the far side of a large fallen rowan tree, then continue alongside the right-hand hedge until another stile and footbridge lead into the next field. A worn path develops which now bears left, still alongside the hedge, through a gateless gap into another field, where a stone stile on the right by a gate leads on to a track. A few yards along this, on your left, is a narrow enclosed path that leads to Zachariah Brow on Saccary Lane.

Go to your left to a stile up some stone steps on your right, at the end of a row of cottages. Follow a worn path that bears right across the field to a gap-stile in a corner, then go along a short length of track to your right and pass through another gap-stile. Cross the next two fields diagonally, corner to corner, climbing all the while, leaving the second by a stone-stepped stile in a short section of wall. Continue in the same direction to reach the triangulation point of Mellor Moor summit, via a stile in the wire fence. This is an exceptionally good view-point if the visibility is good, where time can be spent identifying an endless list of places.

Mellor Moor to the Windmill or the Fieldens Arms.
Leave the summit by following the fence that goes west-
wards, passing on your right a small concrete structure.
Ignore the first stile in the fence, but then cross the stile
in the corner and continue downhill, with Samlesbury airfield on your left front; join Abott Brow by a stile in the
bottom right-hand corner. Go left, then leave the road by
a track on the right after a row of cottages. Just before
Wards Farm (stone house at the end of the track), enter
the field on the left by a stile approached by steps. Follow
the right-hand fence over another stile, then bear left up
the hill, diagonally across the field, to a stile in the far
corner. Follow a fence to the right for a short distance
crossing another stile in a small corner, then keep the same
direction alongside a left-hand wall at first, following a
worn path. Before reaching the end of the field, this path
divides and, depending on whether you want to finish at the
Windmill Hotel or the Fieldens Arms, you will either go
straight on or bear right.

To reach the **Windmill Hotel,** keep straight on to leave
the field by a gap-stile at a gateway. Here, an enclosed
path brings you out opposite Church Lane in Mellor. Turn
right and go down Mellor Brow to a stile on the left, which
is by a gate set back from the road after No. 47. Follow
the right-hand hedge downhill to a stile by a gate, then go
right and left to enter Brundhurst Farm yard, with Lower
Brundhurst Farm over on your left. Leave the yard by a
stile at the bottom end; then, after crossing a narrow field,
enter a large one and continue downhill parallel to an iron
fence over on your left. Leave by a gateway in the bottom
corner, then go right, alongside a hedge, until you reach
the road; the Windmill Hotel is to your right.

If you wish to finish at the **Fieldens Arms,** take the worn
path that bears right, to join the field boundary, which you
keep on your left until you come to a stile after passing a
gate. Over the stile bear right, with the remains of Elswick
weaving mill over on your left. Join the hedge on your
right, at the corner where it bends away, and follow it
downhill in the direction of Longsight Road. At the end
of the second field, a concealed gap-stile leads along a short
stony enclosed path into the next field. Aim across this to
join the main road at a gap-stile in the right-hand corner.
The Fieldens Arms is nearly ½ mile to your left.

A circular walk from Myerscough Arms, near Samlesbury airfield, via Mercyfield Wood.   **6¼ miles.**

No bus service.   Map O.S. 2½" sheet SD 63.

CONTRASTING with the flat area which was chosen for the site of Samlesbury airfield is the hilly nature of the surrounding countryside.   On the north side the land falls away to the River Ribble and, because of this, travellers along the Whalley road do not get a comprehensive look at a rich countryside well endowed with woods and streams.

Myerscough Arms to Mercyfield Wood.   The Myerscough Arms is situated about 1¼ miles along the Whalley road from the junction near The Trafalgar.   On the nearside of the inn is a section of the old road, and leading off this is a farm road.   This leads to Rigby Fold where you pass to the right-hand side of the house by way of a narrow enclosed path, stiled at each end.   Keep down the left-hand side of the field beyond, but before reaching the bottom corner, cross an iron rail to enter the next field at a waterlogged area.   Cut across the right-hand corner to leave at a stile halfway along the bottom boundary, then go forward to a hidden stile just down the slope at the bottom of the field on the left of a ditch.   Continue forward, crossing Bezza Brook at a footbridge.

Climb the bank and pass to the left of Pickering's farmhouse to enter the yard.   On the right, facing the house, is a small brick building at the start of the farm road. Climb the gate on the right just after this building and follow the right-hand hedge almost to the end of the field before crossing the hedge (no stile at time of writing). Continue on the other side of the hedge through two fields, then go diagonally down the next field to join the road at the bottom of Woods Brow after passing between a barn and the white-walled Wilcock Brook Farm.

Cross directly to an old ornamental gate and keep forward through four fields with Wilcock Brook (called Bezza Brook downstream) on your right.   Near the end of the fourth field, bear up the bank to cross a rail-stile (overgrown at the time of writing).   Keep above Richmond Wood in the next field, then bear left after crossing the trace of an old field boundary, to reach Jackson's Banks Road at another ornamental gate on the nearside of a pond.

Follow the road to the right, then fork left at the junction with Commons Lane and go along Nightfield Lane. After passing Nightfield Gate Farm (dated 1747) with its roadside rockery, the road bends left, right and left again. Leave the lane on this last bend at a stiled gateway on the right. There are good views from this spot across the Ribble Valley of Longridge Fell and beyond. Go down two fields with Mercyfield Wood on the right, then enter the wood where it forms a corner at a stile, and follow a faint narrow steep path that descends to a stream. After fording this, climb the opposite bank, again following a faint narrow path that follows a ridge. When the ground

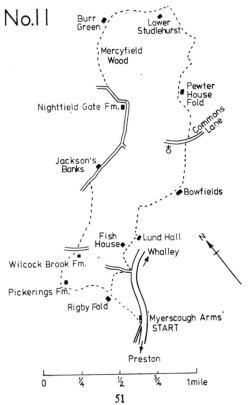

No.11

Burr Green
Lower Studlehurst
Mercyfield Wood
Pewter House Fold
Nightfield Gate Fm.
Commons Lane
Jackson's Banks
Bowfields
Fish House
Lund Hall
Whalley
Wilcock Brook Fm.
Pickerings Fm.
Rigby Fold
Myerscough Arms START
N
Preston

0   ¼   ½   ¾   1mile

51

levels out, bear right and search for a stile that leads out of the wood into a field, where you go right, alongside the wood to a stiled gateway in the corner.

Mercyfield Wood to Myerscough Arms.   A disused water-logged track starts in the next field and leads to the barn and house at Burr Green where the route can be continued by the farm road.   (The actual right-of-way is across the field on the right to pass by the old windpump and rejoin the farm road further on).   The next farm is the renovated Lower Studlehurst, after which ignore a farm road that goes off to Middle Studlehurst, but then look out for a footbridge which crosses the roadside ditch on the right.   Over this, go down the right-hand side of three fields to leave by a footbridge in the corner.

Just before the footbridge is Sandiford Well in a hollow, which could indicate that there was once a settlement in the vicinity; it is interesting to note that in the two fields connected by the footbridge, there are indications of former disturbances. After crossing the footbridge, keep down the left-hand side of the next field, to leave at the furthermost left-hand corner.   When you reach the enclosure of Pewter House Fold in the next field, skirt round to the right until you reach a gate at the end of the field that leads into the yard.

Join the farm road that leads off to the right and follow it a short way to reach a barn on the right.   Turn left here, then cross a stile on the right and go past the end of a cottage.   Bear left to a stiled gateway and pass to the left of a barn to reach two gates in the field corner. Cross the stile by the left-hand gate; then, after a short length of right-hand hedge, bear right to a stile near the diagonal corner.   Continue with a wooded brook on the left to reach Commons Lane opposite Balderstone post-box with the church along to the right.

Little Ease is across the road and a drive starts here that leads up to Balderstone Grange, where you keep right. After about 300 yards the drive bends at Bowfields and becomes a track.   When the track bends left, keep forward over a stiled gateway to a rail stile at the end of the next field. Over this stile, follow the hedge that goes left through two fields to leave the second by a stile a short distance from the corner.   Descend to cross Mellor Brook at a bridge made of large stone slabs and climb up a broad grass track towards Lund Hall.

Leave the track when you are about halfway up to the house, by bearing right above the steep bank of the brook; here you will discover a stile sandwiched between a hedge and a barbed-wire fence. Beyond these bear left across the hillside to pass above a brick tank, then cut across a field to join the farm road (bounded by a hedge) that comes from Fish House over on the right (if no stile has been provided, use the gate in the left-hand corner). Follow the farm road to the left to reach a minor road close to the main road; this can be followed to the right for one-third of a mile to reach the Myerscough Arms.

For those who wish to avoid walking along the main road, there is a slightly longer alternative route. Turn right along the minor road to the main ornamental gateway on the left. Through this, go past Moorhouse Fold (dated I.D. 1690), then turn left in the field beyond, aiming for Rigby Fold which is at the end of the second field. Cross the rail in the corner that leads on to the enclosed path used earlier in the walk and follow the farm road to the Myerscough Arms.

No. 12   DEBT TO CONSERVATIONISTS

A circular walk from Grimsargh Church via Tun Brook. (alternatively, finish at Moor Nook).   **4¼ miles.**

Bus to Grimsargh Church.   Map O.S. 2½″ sheet SD 63.

STAUNCH opposition by conservationists helped to save Tun Brook valley from being overwhelmed by a flood of development; let us hope that it will always remain wild and wooded.

From the church, walk up towards the railway bridge to reach Ribblesdale Drive on the right. Down this, Black-leach Avenue on the right leads to open ground, where you bear right to cross a stiled footbridge in the right-hand hedge. Turn left, following a hedge until you reach another footbridge in the corner, ignoring a culverted bridge on the way. Cross the footbridge and again follow the left-hand hedge to a third footbridge almost at the end of the field; here the banking drops away steeply and the bridge may be difficult to see for vegetation. Over the bridge, follow

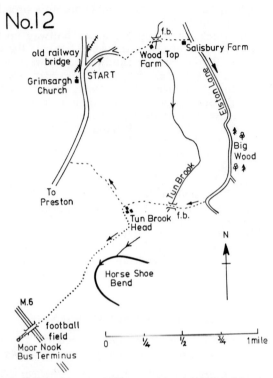

No.12

old railway bridge

Grimsargh Church

START

f.b.

Wood Top Farm

Salisbury Farm

Elston Lane

Big Wood

To Preston

Tun Brook

Tun Brook Head

f.b.

N

Horse Shoe Bend

M.6

football field

Moor Nook Bus Terminus

0   ¼   ½   ¾   1mile

a right-hand hedge to cross a fourth footbridge behind Wood Top Farm.

Join the road at the garden in front of the farm and go left a few yards to some primitive steps on the right, concealed by foliage in summer. These help you to descend the steep wooded bank of Tun Brook, which is crossed by a footbridge. Climb the opposite bank to a stile, then cross the narrow end of a field to another stile. Aim to the right of a tree-lined pond to reach a stile well down the next field in the right-hand hedge. Over this, aim for the cabins over on the left and go around them to join Elston Lane via the farm road of Salisbury Farm. Go right, and after a little over ½ mile the road bends right and left, passing alongside Big Wood. Ignore the road going off left at the end of the wood, keeping on past the gate of Place

House Farm to where the road bends sharp left. Climb the stile in the right-hand corner and cross the field diagonally left, passing a lone tree on the left, to a stile in the left-hand hedge leading into Tun Brook Wood.

The path through the wood, which is easy to find, crosses the brook and leads up to a stile. In the field beyond, cross a stile in the left-hand hedge, almost 70 yards from the wood. Over this, bear slightly right to climb a stile across the field, then bear away from the left-hand hedge to cross a stile in the corner of an extended part of the field on the right of Tunbrook Head Farm. If you want to finish the walk at Grimsargh church, follow the farm road to the right until it bends sharply. A stile here leads on to an enclosed path to Longridge Road; Grimsargh church is to the right. For Moor Nook, go past Tunbrook Head Farm, then turn left along a stiled track that leads above the wooded escarpment of Horse Shoe Bend. Cross a stile at the end of the track and turn right to enter the football field. A cindered track goes down the right-hand side and then the way is over the motorway bridge; the bus terminus is across the road.

No. 13   OLD HIGHWAYS

A circular walk from Potters Lane, Samlesbury, via Dean Lane.   **4¼ miles — shorter version 2 miles.**

Bus to Potters Lane. Maps O.S. 2½" sheets SD 53, 62 and 63.

MODERN mechanised traffic demands high-speed routes, and consequently sections of old highways are continuously being superseded by modern roads. Mellowed by nature, the abandoned roads often make a valuable contribution to our footpath network, as will be seen on this walk. Of the nineteen persons brought to trial at Lancaster in 1612 for witchcraft, eight of them were from Samlesbury — all eight were acquitted.

Shorter Version. From Preston, Potters Lane is on the left of the dual carriageway beyond the two roundabout links with the M6 motorway. Follow the lane past the church of St. Leonard the Less, part of which dates back to the 14th century. After half-a-mile you reach the farm road on the left leading to Seed House Farm and on the opposite side of the road is a track.

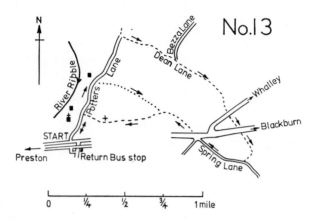

Turn up the track, which is bordered by trees, and keep
to the track when it goes through a left-hand gateway and
then climbs to enter a sloping field. A faint trace of the
track keeps close to the right-hand boundary and enters
the next field at a gate. Follow the left-hand hedge to leave
at a stiled gateway, then go forward until you reach a stile
in the left-hand hedge; this is where the longer version of
the walk joins the shorter one.

Do not cross the stile but turn your back to it and go
over the stile you see ahead. A right-hand fence leads to
another stile, beyond which a green track enters a wood,
running parallel to the main road; this will bring you to
St. Mary's church. At the far end of the church garden,
turn right, through a short length of overgrown path, to
cross a stiled gateway, and then go down the left-hand
side of a sloping field to reach Potters Lane. The section
of path just walked through the wood and down the field
is an old road that led to the Boat House, where a ferry
used to operate. Turn left along Potters Lane to reach the
main road; for the most convenient bus-stop for Preston,
cross the east-bound carriageway and follow Vicarage Lane
under the west-bound section and up the path and steps on
the left to a bus shelter.

Longer Version. Start as in the shorter version, but
follow Potters Lane for almost a mile until you reach a

junction. A farm road (which you do not use) continues ahead to Lower Hall Farm, which stands on the site of the original Samlesbury Hall, destroyed in the 14th century by Robert Bruce. Samlesbury Old Hall or Upper Hall was built on what was then a more secluded site as a replacement for the one destroyed. Your way is to turn up Dean Lane on the right. Bezza Brook is on the right at first, then keep right at a junction, after which the way becomes rough as it first climbs and then levels out to reach Whalley Road. Cross straight over to a stiled gateway and follow the left-hand hedge to Blackburn New Road.

Again, cross straight over to a gate, through which go forward to another gate. Then follow a line of trees and a gulley downhill. This boundary bears right and brings you to a footbridge over Hole Brook. Cross it, then cut across a bend and go alongside the stream to reach Spring Lane. This road, followed to the right, will bring you back to the main road opposite the Trafalgar. Cross over and go left to a stile at the end of the car-park, which leads onto an old track around a field.

Follow the boundary round until you leave the field at a stile in the far corner adjacent to a high concrete wall on the left; go alongside this and cross a facing stile (not the one on the left). The stile crossed is the one mentioned on the shorter version already described.

No. 14   **SILVER HOARD**

Circular walk from Halfpenny Bridge, via Cuerdale.
4 miles — shorter route 2 miles.

Bus to Farringdon Park terminus. Maps O.S. 2½″ sheets SD 52 and 53. (If the walk is started and finished at the Farringdon Park bus terminus, a total of one mile will be added. If preferred, this walk can be started and finished at Mill Tavern near Cann Bridge, Higher Walton; for this alternative, start by walking along the main road towards Preston and turn to the paragraph in the text headed "Higher Walton to Halfpenny Bridge").

EXTENSIVE views in clear conditions can be had on this walk, as the route traverses the ridge between the Ribble and Darwen valleys. By the Ribble at Cuerdale is a stone marking the site where the historic Cuerdale Hoard was found.

Farringdon Park to Higher Walton. Walk down the footway on the right-hand side of the main road at Brockholes Brow, past the Royal Cross School and cross the river Ribble at Brockholes (Halfpenny) Bridge. Leave the road by a gap-stile on the right at the end of the bridge, where a flight of steps descends to join the riverside path. After ¼ mile a small wooded stream is crossed at a bridge, beyond which leave the riverside as you cut diagonally left across a field to a stile part-way down the top boundary. In the next field, aim for a stile in the top right-hand corner adjacent to the motorway. Over this stile, continue in the field alongside the motorway, until you join Cuerdale Lane at a stile.

If you wish to do the **shorter version,** go along the lane to your right, passing Webster's Farm on the right and Wood House Farm on the left, and then turn down the farm road on the right, where the road bends left. This leads downhill through Cuerdale Wood and the yard of Cuerdale Hall Farm to the river bank which, if you follow it to your right, will bring you back to Halfpenny Bridge. (About 400 yards downstream from where the footpath joins the river bank at Cuerdale Hall Farm is the stone marking the spot where the Cuerdale Hoard was found in 1840. This is thought to be the largest single amount of silver to be unearthed in this country, and one theory is that it was left behind by the Scandinavians and allies after their defeat at the battle of Brunabergh (various spellings) in 937 A.D. Permission to see the stone must be obtained from the farm).

For the **longer version,** turn left along Cuerdale Lane to a stiled gateway on the right just after you have crossed the motorway bridge. After a length of track another stiled gateway leads into a field which you leave in the far diagonal corner. Cross over an access road to another stile beyond which, on your right, is the perimeter fence of a North Sea Gas site. At the end of the site, turn right and head for a stile in line with the tall silage container at Sallom House. Leave the next field at a gate in the far diagonal corner, adjacent to the farm buildings, and then go through the gate on your left. Follow the field

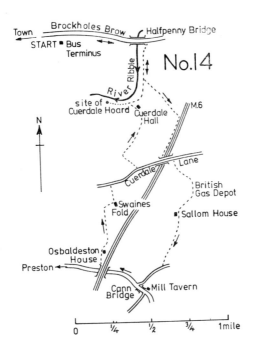

boundary to your right, to cross a stile in the corner. Keep to the left-hand hedge, over the crown of the hill, with All Saints church, Higher Walton, directly ahead; you are now at the top of the ridge that divides the Ribble and Darwen rivers. Join a track at the bottom of the hill and keep forward to a junction, where you turn right, over a cattle grid, and continue along Banister Hall Lane; this leads to the main road at Higher Walton via Shop Lane, with Cann Bridge, over the river Darwen, just to your left.

Higher Walton to Halfpenny Bridge. Turn right along the main road (it may be safer to walk on the opposite side); then, after passing under the motorway bridge, turn up the rough road on your right, signposted "Cuerdale Lane." This leads to the fine old Osbaldeston House dated 1661. Leave the yard by a gate in the far right-hand corner, and then climb the banking ahead and to the left. Keep to the right-hand boundary around two sides of the field and leave it at a double stile in the second corner. Three-quarters of the way down the next field, go through a gate on the right and follow the right-hand hedge to Swains Fold, where a stile leads on to the access road.

Cuerdale Lane is to the left, along which you go to the right, until you reach a rough road on the left where the lane bends right. This is the way to Cuerdale Hall Farm and Halfpenny Bridge, as described in the shorter version of the walk above.

No. 15   HEAD FOR THE MARSHES

A circular walk from the Golden Ball, Longton, via the Flying Fish.   **5½ miles.**

Bus to the Golden Ball.   Map O.S. 2½″ sheet SD 42.

FOR a change, turn your back on to the hills and head for the marshes; no hills to climb, a completely different outlook and where could the air be fresher?

Golden Ball to the Flying Fish. The Golden Ball stands at the junction of Liverpool Road and Marsh Lane. Cross over the start of Marsh Lane and go a few yards in the Preston direction to a track that goes off between hedges on the left. This takes you through to Back Lane, a metalled road, where a few yards to the right you will find a stile on the left. This leads on to a length of enclosed path and then continues along a right-hand hedge. In the next field, bear left to meet Longton Brook; turn left and go alongside the brook until you come to a footbridge at the end of the following field.

Cross the brook and follow the right-hand hedge around two sides of a field (ignoring the field bridge in the first corner) to a stile in the second corner. Over the stile, continue in the same direction to cross a footbridge, then bear right, aiming for a point 20 yards to the right of a pylon, to cross a wooden fence followed by a plank bridge (ignore the wooden stile a few feet from where you cross). Follow the right-hand hedge to cross a stile in the corner by a trough, then turn left to reach Grange Lane on the right of a large fuel-tank.

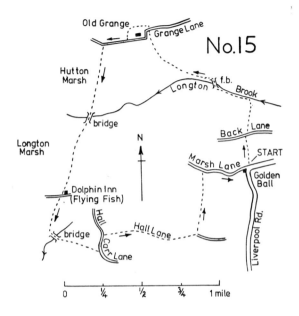

You now have to get past Old Grange, the farm down the road to your left; this entails a detour. Turn right along the lane (farm road) as far as a gate on the left at the end of a small wood. Through the gate, turn sharp left, aiming to the right-hand corner of the farm buildings. Pass along the top side of these, then keep forward to meet a line of trees; turn left on the other side of these and follow them to regain Grange Lane at a gate. (N.B.: At the time of writing, there is a single strand of barbed wire to negotiate at the line of trees).

Turn right along the lane to where it bends slightly at a gateway, and then go through the left of two opposite gates flanking the lane. This leads into a field $\frac{1}{2}$ mile long, where the right-of-way runs at varying distances from the left-hand boundary. At first it is 20 yards away widening to about 55 yards; by the halfway stage the gap has narrowed a little to 40 yards and you leave the field at a gate about 80 yards to the right of the far corner. Go through the gate, re-cross Longton Brook by the right-hand of two bridges, and go through another gate. Some distance ahead is a

61

clay-pigeon tower. Aim for this, through yet another gate, then across a field to join a right-hand fence that leads to a rail-stile in the corner. Over this, carry on past the tower to reach Marsh Lane at the end of a length of track; the Dolphin Inn (known locally as the Flying Fish) is just to your left.

Flying Fish to the Golden Ball. Cross straight over and continue by a track alongside a renovated cottage. The track becomes grassy and ends in a field, where you follow the left-hand fence until an embankment is reached, just beyond a stile. Go a few yards along the top of the embankment and keep left when it divides; this brings you to a bridge and flood-gates, at what is called Tarra Carr Gutter, which runs into the river Douglas just over to the right.

Cross the stile on the bridge and continue along the embankment for about 60 yards until it bends right, then leave it and follow a hedge that has started on the left. When this hedge bends left, keep forward under the high-tension wires to rejoin the embankment, which you follow until it is crossed by a fence. Turn left a few yards to a gate leading on to Hall Carr Lane (a metalled road).

Turn left along the lane for about 200 yards to a junction with white railings, where you fork right into Hall Lane. After a house the lane becomes an enclosed green track; later, beyond a sewerage works, the way becomes stony and then metalled after passing a short terrace of houses on the right. Leave the lane here at an enclosed path on the left; this goes past the car-park of the industrialised Oak House Farm on the right and leads to a stile and foot-bridge to re-cross Tarra Carr Gutter.

Do not cross the stile on the right in the field corner, but go forward through a gap into the next field, and then make for the left-hand hedge and follow it to an iron step-ladder stile. Over this, continue along a well-worn enclosed path to reach Marsh Lane via the drive of a house and a wicket gate; the Golden Ball is one-third of a mile to the right.

No. 16   MESSING ABOUT DOWN THE RIVER

Freckleton to Lytham. 5½ miles.
(alternatively, finish at Wrea Brook — 4¼ miles).

*Bus to the Coach and Horses, Freckleton. Maps O.S.
2½" sheets SD 32, 42 and 43.*

THIS AREA is the haunt of wild-fowlers, bird-watchers,
boatmen and fishermen, each finding scope to pursue his
own recreation in a vast expanse of river and marsh. High
tides will test your ingenuity in negotiating the route, so be
prepared for a challenge.

Freckleton to Naze Point. From the bus-stop, walk past
the Coach and Horses down Preston Old Road until Bunker Street on the right is reached. Here you must decide
whether to take the top or bottom path alongside Freckleton Pool. For the **top path,** turn down Bunker Street
which goes by the Ship Inn (in former times associated with
smugglers and sail-making). After some cottages the way
narrows down to become a footpath along the top of a
wooded embankment that stretches out for a mile to reach
the river at Naze Point. Because of the flat nature of the
surrounding area, the embankment is a prominent feature
for miles around and, for the same reason, extensive views
can be had on clear days. Before reaching the river, a
detour has to be made around Naze Cottage garden by way
of an enclosed path that leads into a field; keep to the right-
hand side of this, then go down the embankment to reach
the riverside opposite the estuary of the river Douglas. In
1882 there was a scheme to cross the Ribble at this point
by a railway, but Preston Corporation (concerned about
restrictions to navigation) opposed the idea; later schemes
were abandoned because of high costs.

If you wish to reach Naze Point by the interesting but
sticky **bottom path,** turn off Preston Old Road immediately
after passing Bunker Street, to reach Dow Brook which
runs through Freckleton Pool. Follow the rough road to
the right, past Pool House Stables and through the boat-
yard to reach Pool House Farm. At the yard entrance a
small gate on the left enables you to pass between the pool
and the farm; then the way continues past two renovated

dwellings, quaintly nicknamed the "Dolls Houses" to reach the river at Naze Point, close to where the alternative route reaches the Ribble.

Naze Point to Lytham Dock. From here the route to Lytham Dock is either along or alongside the embankment on the inland fringe of the marshland bordering the river. After about ¾ mile, Pool Stream is crossed at a hand-railed footbridge (this is shortly beyond where Pool Lane runs down to the marsh).

A short distance after crossing the footbridge, when the perimeter fence of Warton airfield is close on the right, you are near to the site of Guides' House, from where people were guided across the river to Hesketh Bank — the journey could also be made on horseback. Before the last war there was a caravan site here where people came from Preston and further afield, many on foot, to spend their annual holiday.

Continue along the top of the embankment, past the airfield until you reach a stile leading on to a track, which is followed towards a white house and past a present-day caravan site at Warton Bank. The area between Warton Bank and Lytham is thought at one time to have been covered by a forest, a theory confirmed last century when one hundred trees were brought up during dredging operations in the river channel.

Beyond a gate the way is again along the embankment until you reach Brook Cottage on the nearside of Wrea Brook. Lack of a footbridge at this point means a detour to the main road to cross Brook Bridge. If you wish to end the walk here, the Preston bus-stop is to the left on the far side of the road. To continue the walk, leave the road and come back along the other side of Wrea Brook; then the embankment will lead you a further 1¼ miles to reach the road at Lytham Dock.

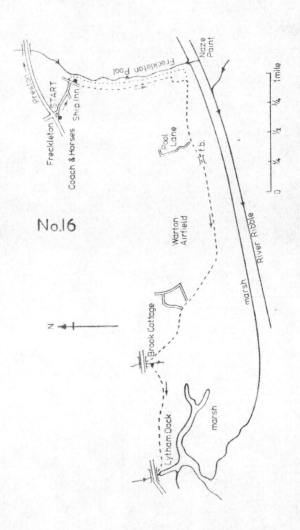

No.16